FAR

The Great Piano Works Of
EDVARD GRIEG

D0732122

WARNER BROS. PUBLICATIONS - THE GLOBAL LEADER IN PRINT
USA: 15800 NW 48th Avenue, Miami, FL 33014

WARNER/CHAPPELL MUSIC

CANADA: 85 SCARSDALE ROAD, SUITE 101
DON MILLS, ONTARIO, M3B 2R2
SCANDINAVIA: P.O. BOX 533, VENDEVAGEN 85 B
S-182 15, DANDERYD, SWEDEN
AUSTRALIA: P.O. BOX 353
3 TALAVERA ROAD, NORTH RYDE N.S.W. 2113

NUOVA CARISCH

ITALY: VIA M.F. QUINTILIANO 40
20138 MILANO
SPAIN: MAGALLANES, 25
28015 MADRID

INTERNATIONAL MUSIC PUBLICATIONS LIMITED

ENGLAND: SOUTHEND ROAD,
WOODFORD GREEN, ESSEX IG8 8HN
FRANCE: 25 RUE DE HAUTEVILLE, 75010 PARIS
GERMANY: MARSTALLISTR. 8, D-80539 MUNCHEN
DENMARK: DANMUSIK, VOGNMAGERGADE 7
DK 1120 KOBENHAVNK

Project Manager: Dale Tucker
Design: Michael Ramsay

EDVARD GRIEG
Born: June 15, 1843-Bergen, Norway
Died: September 4, 1907-Bergen, Norway

Edvard Grieg was born to musical parents in Norway on June 15, 1843. His father played the piano moderately well, but his mother was considered a gifted pianist and singer who had performed with orchestras in their city of Bergen. She was Edvard's first music teacher, and from her he developed his intense love for music. Grieg had a great interest in poetry as a boy and often spoke of being a poet or a minister when he grew up. He was not considered a good student, academically or musically, as he was lazy about his studies and practice schedule.

Grieg began composing as a young boy, but his compositions were not taken seriously until he was in his early teen years. A visit to the Grieg home by noted violinist and composer, Ole Bull, exposed the first recognition of Grieg's true talent. Bull saw and heard some of 15-year old Edvard's compositions, and persuaded his parents to send him to the Leipzig Conservatory. There, his health suffered and took him away from his studies for a time, but he returned, winning honors in composition and piano until he graduated in 1862.

As a composer, Grieg often felt uninspired, and considered himself unsuccessful. However he began to write music inspired by his native Norway, giving the world insight into this lovely country and its people. This proved to be a positive avenue for him, although it was some time before works were performed and he was accepted as a noted musician. Among those who appreciated his writing was Franz Liszt, and also a cousin, whom he later married, who was a singer. For her he composed many songs.

In general his piano works are not difficult, his songs are lovely and reflective of his native land, and his orchestral works are still often performed today. He also became a successful orchestra conductor, and toured Europe in this position. Grieg was awarded many honors during his life, including honorary Doctorates from Cambridge and Oxford Universities.

Grieg suffered a heart attack in early September, 1907 and died only two days later. As a final honor, his body lay in state following his death, and thousands came to pay a final tribute.

CONTENTS

5

PEER GYNT SUITE NO. 1

Opus 46

I.

MORNING MOOD

EDVARD GRIEG

II.
THE DEATH OF THE ASS

Andante doloroso ♩ = 50.

III.
ANITRA'S DANCE

Tempo di Mazurka ♩ = 160

IV.
IN THE HALL OF THE MOUNTAIN KING

sempre stretto al fine

POETIC TONE-PICTURE

Opus 3, No. 4

POETIC TONE-PICTURE

Opus 3, No. 5

WALTZ IN A MINOR

Opus 12, No. 2

WATCHMAN'S SONG

Opus 12, No. 3

ELFIN DANCE

Opus 12, No. 4

Molto allegro e sempre staccato

FOLK SONG

Opus 12, No. 5

NORWEGIAN MELODY

Opus 12, No. 6

ALBUM LEAF

Opus 12, No. 7

NATIONAL SONG

Opus 12, No. 8

HUMORESQUE

Opus 6, No. 3

DANCE CAPRICE

Opus 28, No. 3

ALBUM LEAF

Opus 28, No. 4

Andantino serioso

p la melodia ben tenuta

mf

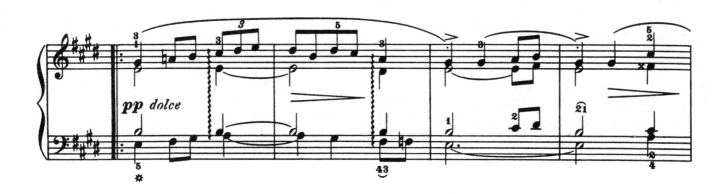

pp dolce

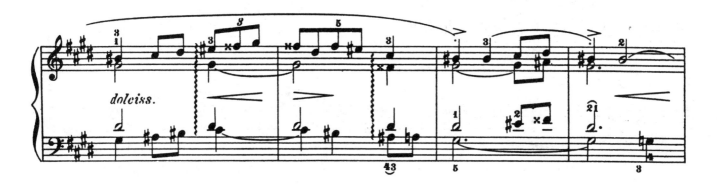

dolciss.

WALTZ IN E MINOR

Opus 34, No. 7

THE LAST SPRING

Opus 34, No. 2

BERCEUSE

Opus 38, No. 1

Con moto

FOLK SONG

Opus 38, No. 2

SPRING DANCE

Opus 38, No. 5

ELEGIE

Opus 38, No. 6

Allegretto semplice

WALTZ

Opus 38, No. 7

BUTTERFLY

Opus 43, No. 1

This page has been left blank to avoid awkward page turns.

THE LONELY WANDERER

Opus 43, No. 2

NATIVE LAND

Opus 43, No. 3

LITTLE BIRD

Opus 43, No. 4

EROTIK

Opus 43, No. 5

VALSE-IMPROMPTU

Opus 47, No. 1

ALBUM LEAF

Opus 47, No. 2

Allegro vivace e grazioso

MELODIE IN A MINOR

Opus 47, No. 3

This page has been left blank to avoid awkward page turns.

MELANCHOLIE

Opus 47, No. 5

ELEGIE

Opus 47, No. 7

RINGING BELLS

Opus 54, No. 6

HOME-SICKNESS

Opus 57, No. 6

Molto più vivo

GRATITUDE

Opus 62, No. 2

PEASANT'S SONG

Opus 65, No. 2

BALLADE IN C MINOR

Opus 65, No. 5

This page has been left blank to avoid awkward page turns.

SAILOR'S SONG

Opus 68, No. 1

GRANDMOTHER'S MINUET

Opus 68, No. 2

Allegretto grazioso e leggierissimo

AT THY FEET

Opus 68, No. 3

PUCK

Opus 71, No. 3

This page has been left blank to avoid awkward page turns.

REMEMBERANCES

Opus 71, No. 7

NORWEGIAN DANCE

Opus 17, No. 2

HOLBERG SUITE

Opus 40

I.

PRELUDE

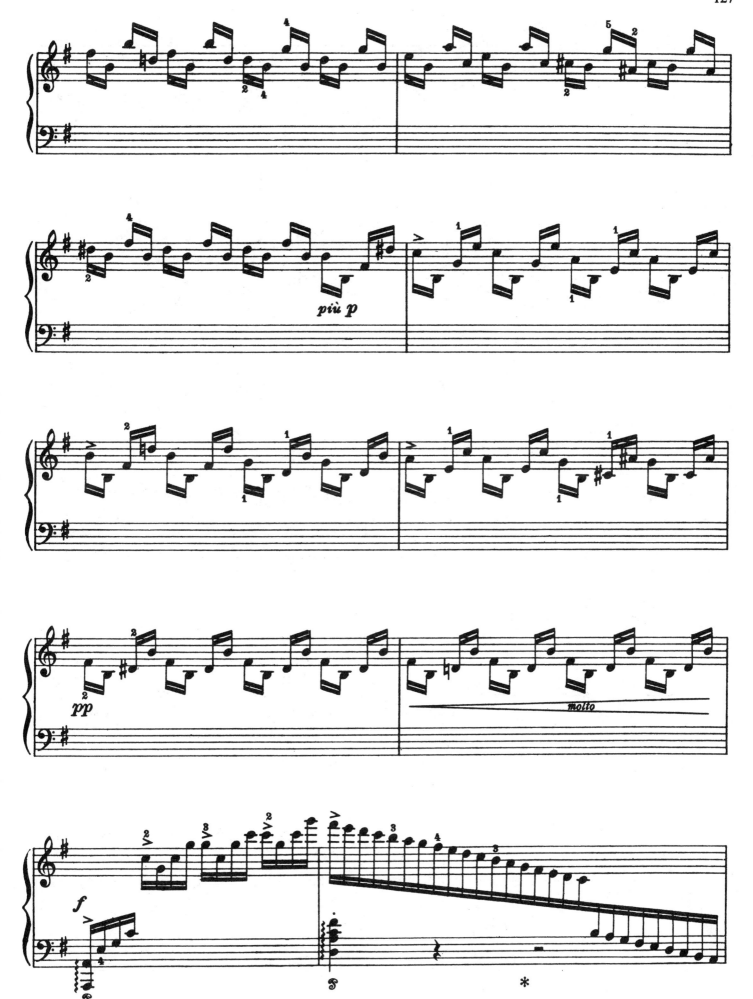

II.
SARABANDE

Andante espressivo ♩=52

III.
GAVOTTE

Musette
Un poco più mosso

Gavotte d.c. sin' al fine

IV.
AIR

V.
RIGAUDON

Rigaudon d. c. sin' al fine
ma senza repetizione

OPENING THEME

(from the First Movement of the Piano Concerto)